THIS IS ME! 2022

HERE I COME

Edited By Lynsey Evans

First published in Great Britain in 2022 by:

Young Writers
Remus House
Coltsfoot Drive
Peterborough
PE2 9BF
Telephone: 01733 890066
Website: www.youngwriters.co.uk

All Rights Reserved
Book Design by Ashley Janson
© Copyright Contributors 2022
Softback ISBN 978-1-80015-972-3

Printed and bound in the UK by BookPrintingUK
Website: www.bookprintinguk.com
YB0504N

FOREWORD

For Young Writers' latest competition This Is Me, we asked primary school pupils to look inside themselves, to think about what makes them unique, and then write a poem about it! They rose to the challenge magnificently and the result is this fantastic collection of poems in a variety of poetic styles.

Here at Young Writers our aim is to encourage creativity in children and to inspire a love of the written word, so it's great to get such an amazing response, with some absolutely fantastic poems. It's important for children to focus on and celebrate themselves and this competition allowed them to write freely and honestly, celebrating what makes them great, expressing their hopes and fears, or simply writing about their favourite things. This Is Me gave them the power of words. The result is a collection of inspirational and moving poems that also showcase their creativity and writing ability.

I'd like to congratulate all the young poets in this anthology, I hope this inspires them to continue with their creative writing.

CONTENTS

Independent Entries

Polina Chuykov (10)	1
Avneet Kaur Saria (10)	2
Abdurrahman Abbas (10)	5
Gurkirat Kaur Saria (12)	6
Ava Walters (9)	9
Vikashini Vinodh (10)	10
Kanista Wickneshwaran (11)	12
Keziah Pothin (10)	14
Omaira Gupta Anand (8)	16
Meera Jassal (7)	18
George Frank Gamble (8)	20
Sumaya Omar (10)	22
Maya Rose Pugh (8)	25
Tyler Forshaw-Abrahams (9)	26
Rhea Chowdhury (10)	28
Alfie Clark (10)	30
Clara Uddin (11)	32
Diya Purewal (9)	34
Aaliya Kaidi (10)	36
Troy Dennis (10)	38
Mia Tongson (8)	40
Lucy-Marie Phillips (11)	42
Izzy Howe (9)	44
Bethany Hood (9)	46
Naima Murshida	48
Shiv Dev (9)	50
Amelia Connolly (8)	52
Lola Gardner (9)	54
Arnav Ghoshal (10)	56
Evelyn Edwards (11)	58
Ramin Ahmed (9)	59
Archie Wootton	60
Hway Cheng (7)	62
Nico Worswick-Hogwood (8)	64
Kaitlyn Leung (10)	66
Shofei Shanthakumar (9)	68
Maheen Fahad (11)	70
Fred Gamble (7)	71
Scarlett Bartholomew (10)	72
Brooke Nicolette LoPinto	75
Hoda Ahmed (11)	76
Isla Joliat (9)	77
Aisha Ali	78
Oaka Rose Taylor (7)	80
Atiaat Bello	81
Amelie Raine (8)	82
Ralph Mahadevan (3)	83
Isabelle Evans (8)	84
Sofia Dantas (10)	85
Juwayriyah Noor (9)	86
Utkarsh Gupta (11)	87
Louisa Schock (8)	88
Kira Pau (8)	90
Parshva Mehta (8)	91
Memphis Morris (10)	92
Daniel Houghton (8)	93
Molly Kennedy (9)	94
Beatrice Clark	95
Isla Foden-Reekie (9)	96
Marina Rutherford	97
Seren Bowen	98
Angelina Dhir (11)	99
Felicity Payton (10)	100
Bethlehem Bereket (9)	101
Musa Chowdhury (8)	102
Luqman Lockwood (9)	104
Nikita Padki	105
Lana Reza (8)	106
Leo Assad (9)	108

Name	Page
Ella Brophy (9)	109
Oliver King (11)	110
Ethan Parker (11)	111
Otto Cheffers Gibbs (10)	112
Bethan Everett (11)	113
Paige Lewis (8)	114
Alma Miles Herrera (7)	115
Muhammad Ahmed Khan (9)	116
Jasmine Mayne (8)	117
Reneika White (10)	118
Thiviya Kamalendran (10)	119
Simar Kaur (7)	120
Poppy Sandamas (8)	121
Holly Bannister (11)	122
Anu Sathya Umashankar (10)	123
Chloë Alexander (10)	124
Louis Roberts (10)	125
Brody Lineham (10)	126
Hanaa Rashid (7)	127
Malayka Moeed Yazdani (9)	128
Laiba Syed (10)	129
Rose Tappin (10)	130
Ruth George (8)	132
Isabelle Clarke (10)	133
Santosh Tal (9)	134
Genevieve Jefferys (10)	135
Ruhaniya Khalid (8)	136
Enya Smith (8)	138
Safa Hussain (8)	139
Mia King (11)	140
Khatijah Khan (9)	141
Finlay Hudd (11)	142
Talha Patel (7)	143
Annousheh Sayed (8)	144
Sara Szymaniak (11)	145
Madeline Merritt (10)	146
Alice Rowley (8)	147
Mia Opoku Agyeman (9)	148
Haleema Zeeshan (11)	150
Jayden Rowlands (9)	151
Ezekiel Han (9)	152
Ilyas Connelly (9)	153
Amanda Dike (12)	154
Ashley Cunningham (8)	155
Luke Laloux (9)	156
Anisah Haseeb (8)	157
Layan El-Wakhery (10)	158
Saim Yasir (10)	159
Ruby Mae Dignam (9)	160
Kayla Ovadia	162
Mila Patel (9)	163
Cadence Edwards (8)	164
Gulcihan Cakir (9)	165
Felix Pace (9)	166
Abdullah Binn-Omar (10)	167
Iris Perry (9)	168
Lucas Seager (7)	169
Casey Smith	170
Joey Baker (11)	171
Kevin Monu (8)	172
Ishaal Liaqat (6)	173
Bernice Ndu Ariolu	174
Nathan Tang (10)	175
Safiyyah Abubakar (7)	176
Shaylan Patel (11)	177
Marley Jackson (10)	178
Evelyn Thompson (8)	179
Issa Chowdhury (4)	180
Jessica Emberson (7)	181
Lucas M (8)	182
Aiden Chesler (7)	183
Charlotte Walker (5)	184
Poppy Cosgrove (7)	185
Shania Mbaziira (11)	186
Talia Elatta (11)	187
Minudi Thilakarathna (9)	188
Ruby Miller-Barratt (11)	189
Sona Dukkipati (10)	190
Jamie Williams (8)	191
Maryam Iqbal	192
Varenya Sharma (8)	193
Ilinca Maria Istrati (10)	194
Aishlinn Garvey (10)	195
Aimee Kelly (8)	196
James Mason (7)	197
Layla Fitzgerald (8)	198

Abby Bassong (8)	199
Jinxuan Chen (11)	200
Rayne Lucita (9)	201
Keishin Okano (8)	202
Mia Griffin (9)	203
Isabelle Seabrook (10)	204
David Fleming (11)	205
Lola Tash (10)	206

Alder Hey Children's Hospital, Waterloo

Aimee Swart (11)	207

Hassenbrook Academy, Stanford-Le-Hope

Daisy Adela Anderson (12)	208

THE POEMS

This Is Me

The morning began with me waking up late.
I looked at the clock, it was almost eight!
I flew down the stairs, past my half-awake brother
And ran to the kitchen to see my mad mother.
I grabbed my school bag and jumped in the car,
We drove to the school and I had a cereal bar.
Suddenly, I looked down at the uncomfortable seat,
And realised that I had no shoes, just bare feet!
Despite the horrible start to a new week,
It made me realise that every day is unique.
Sometimes you can have a lovely day,
When everyone does what you want, what you say!
And yet some days are a terrible mess,
You can fall off the stairs and rip a new dress.
Days are unique, just like every human being,
Some people like football, others like skiing.
No one is the same, it keeps the world fun!
This is me! I love to read and I often run!
I'm quite good at netball and I also knit.
This is me! I'm special and I love it!

Polina Chuykov (10)

Me And My Grandma

Grandma, you will always be by my side,
With the extraordinary love you provide.
You mean a lot to me,
Even though sometimes we might not agree.

Millions of gifts you have showered upon me,
As we drink tea.
You are my saviour through the dark times,
This is why I have loved you for a long time.

Whenever I need you,
You're always there,
You're like a best friend,
In the air.

Grandma, you're a wonderful grandma,
So gentle, yet so strong.
The many ways you show you care,
Always makes me feel like I belong.

You're patient when I'm foolish,
You give guidance when I ask.

It seems like you can do anything,
You're the master of any tasks.

I love you more than you know,
You have my total respect.
If I had a choice of grandma,
You would be the one I'd select.

There isn't a grandma sweeter,
Than a grandma like you.
One filled with love and laughter,
In anything you do.

I've learned a lot from you through the years,
Oh Grandma, can't you see?
Live, laugh and love
Is what you have taught me.

Baking cookies one by one,
Panting flowers in the sun.
Reading books on her lap,
Cuddling up for a nap.

Long walks in the park,
Watching stars in the dark.

Kissing boo-boos on my knee,
Big squeeze hugs just for me.

Grandma, without you,
Life would be a scary place.
We would miss the
Kindness on your face.

I really feel quite special,
That God has chosen you,
To be the person in my life,
Who knows me through and through.

Love your sweet granddaughter,
Avneet.

Avneet Kaur Saria (10)

This Is About Me

T ackling through the crowd makes me proud, this is me.
H igh up in the air the ball goes, this is me.
I am tall, the rest are small, this is me.
S hining in the sky like a star, this is me.

I scream for ice cream, this is me.
S leeping is what I do best, this is me.

A ccompanied by my fantastic uncles, that are always there for me, this is me.
B ecause the world is against me, I prove them wrong, this is me.
O celots are my favourite cats, this is me.
U p and down with a frown, life is too short, enjoy it while you can, this is me.
T he end is near I fret in despair, this is me.

M ilkshakes are the best, this is me.
E xcitement is something I always have, this is me.

Abdurrahman Abbas (10)

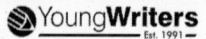

Me And My Wonderful Mother

Mom, you are a wonderful mother,
So gentle, yet so strong.

Without you, there would be no one.

Your love, your attention, your guidance,
Has made me who I am.

Without you, I would be lost,
Wandering aimlessly,
Without direction or purpose.

Every hour, every day,
Makes me so grateful,
That I am yours and you are mine.

Your love protects me day after day,
So I am fearless, safe and sound.

I feel that I can do anything
Whenever you're around.

You are my teacher,
My comforter, my encourager.

The many ways you show you care,
Always makes me feel I belong.

You're patient when I'm foolish,
You give guidance when I ask.

It seems you can do anything,
You're the master of every task.

I appreciate you more,
As the years come and go.

You are always the person I look up to,
So strong, so caring, so loving.

You mean a lot to me,
Even though we might now agree.

I love you more than you know,
You have my total respect.

If I had my choice of mothers,
You'd be the one I'd select.

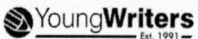

Mothers are priceless,
And I am glad you're mine.

In all the world
There is no mother better than my own.

You're the best and wisest person,
I have ever met.

Whatever I become,
It is because of you...

From your favourite child,
Gurkirat.

Gurkirat Kaur Saria (12)

Sharpen Your Ears

Hello, my name is Ava
And I am here to be a saviour
To the planet, to the animals, to the humans.
This is my mission, this is my song
And I'm here to tell you what we are doing wrong.
So in 2021, we hear of COP26,
Some people think well this is a fix!
But have we acted? Have we taken part?
Sometimes I think we humans have no heart.
Now listen to me now, please listen to my words,
If we don't act now there will be no seas nor birds.
Think of those animals that we love so dearly,
Sharpen your ears, can you hear me clearly?
Listen to David, listen to Greta
And in the end it will all be better.
Now don't think it's just adults
Who can make this choice
Because we, us children, we have a voice.

Ava Walters (9)

This Is Me

Sometimes I am me,
Sometimes I am what people expect to be
They tell me to stop being a childish kid
I feel like I am a kettle about to boil
but captured with a lid
Sometimes I get angry for no reason
But in my mind, I am always thinking
of an excuse, treason
When I get green with jealousy and red with anger
I try not to bite like a fuming vampire
Sometimes I play football and even netball
I'm not small but can be shy enough
to roll into a ball
My brain is ever so smart like Albert Einstein
But still looking for a chance to shine
Sometimes I may be angry but I have a good heart
Some people hate it,
some people think it's sweet as a tart
The bond I have with my family and friends is great
I still think about my own fate
Sometimes I look in the mirror

and look like a huge pile of stink
But who cares about what my parents
and friends think
I have a few pretty friends
But it's what you have inside that counts in the end
Sometimes I am frustrated with my parents,
You know what I mean?
They always like to create a mortifying scene
In the morning, it's 200ml of tiredness
Splashed in my face
And a dash of frustration when I'm tying my lace
Sometimes people always compare me to others
I think it's unfair
How they compare me to my brother
But when I look at myself
I don't compare myself to everyone else
I always will think of my own
great, wonderful success.

Vikashini Vinodh (10)

A Piece Of Blank Paper

There are so many things that I could write
Yet the paper's completely white
While the others scribble away
I'm still stuck on what to say
The others seem to get on all right
So why am I stuck on what to write?
No, need help; guess I'm out of luck
I seem to be one who is clearly stuck
Try as I might, the pen won't move
Something tells me that they won't approve...
The paper remains blank; I still don't have a clue
I didn't expect an idea to come out of the blue
However hard I try, the idea won't come
The pen remains still and my hand goes numb
Though my goals seem hard and very distant
I will continue to be resilient
The others may look at me with a smug smirk
But I'm too distracted to care and my brain starts to work
I gaze down at my paper and start scribbling away
My hand coincidentally begins to do as I say

I continue to write as my confidence
begins to grow
What does it matter if I was a bit slow?
I am now eager to write it all down
Now a smile is on my face instead of a frown
I write this, I write that, I write all about me
Nothing can stop me, as you and they
can clearly see
For one with ideas came up with not many
Believed in herself and came up with plenty
Fill those pages with your beautiful thoughts
You're able to accomplish achievements
of all sorts.

Kanista Wickneshwaran (11)

The Calm Sky Of Knowledge

The calm sky of knowledge
I woke up,
Magnificent, heavenly
Light flowing through the wispy
Clouds, that slowly drift apart,
Presenting a beautiful sky above.
Speaking out to me,
Telling me my purpose,
My priorities,
It gives me knowledge
On every one of my thoughts,
My dreams, my darkest fears.
From then on, I realised who I am.
I'm going to be me, forever.
I feel many emotions,
Positive or negative,
At times I may feel optimistic, bold, proud.
Or weak, pessimistic, dejected.
Shy, composed, ravenous,

But deep down I know I am me.
I admire my talents:
Dancing and acting.
It makes me feel... me.
These people complete me,
They make me feel like
The luckiest person in the world,
They are beautiful, gorgeous and handsome,
Without them, I would be nothing,
I admire their perks,
It makes me look up to them.
I love them with all my heart.
I dream about being a famous actor
Acting in some dancing shows
(Like 'The Next Step'),
Action, adventure, horror and romance movies.
I do know I make mistakes.
My family and teddies
Make me feel cheerful when I am down,
I know exactly who to be.
Unique and different from all,
I would be me.

Keziah Pothin (10)

I'm Unique

I would love to be Prime Minister when I'm older
The whole country would rest on my shoulder

I wouldn't be bossy, oh no, I'd be nice
A click of my finger and jobs being done in a trice

I adore writing; I'm devoted to it
Maybe being a writer will be a marvellous hit

Talking of hobbies, I'm addicted to books
If someone stole them, I'd give them fierce looks

I'm good at most things (I won the Form Prize)
I can do anything, no matter my size

Above are my dreams, below are my fears
Global warming makes me burst into tears

Something is nibbling at my head
It's pollution, animals are dead

Pollution needs to be stopped, now not later
How morose would it be to have an extinct alligator?

Alligators are scary, I admit that
But think about it, it's the same as your cat

I'll solve all the problems when I'm Prime Minister
Some will be small, others will be sinister

Back to the hopes and dreams of my time
If I met my hero, my heart would go chime

"Always stay true to yourself," Michelle Obama said
I will always keep this clearly in my head.

Omaira Gupta Anand (8)

Why So Cheerful?

Many ask why I'm always so cheerful
and with delight.
I say I'm highly blessed is the reason
I give with pride.
For it's the small things in life that please me.
Like my daddy giving me hugs and listening to me.
It's the way my grandma picks me up
and gently places me on her knees.
Telling me stories of her roots and her history.

Many ask why I'm always so sunny and bright.
I say I'm highly blessed is the reason
I give with delight.
For it's the small things in life that please me.
Like going on long nature walks with my family.
It's the way we talk, play and giggle that makes
me beam with glee.

Many ask why I'm always smiling
and easily pleased.
I say I'm highly blessed is the reason I give so
gracefully.

For it's the small things in life that please me.
Like the experiences that I cherish and receive.
From the way I splash in a cool pool, playing games at school
and learning more than one language
are all great life tools.

I'm always happy to appreciate
the small things in life,
especially being a cheerful girl like me.
Yes me!

Meera Jassal (7)

Like A Butterfly

B utterflies impress me. I like their different colours and the shape of their wings.
U nusual things that I like are veggie volcano rolls, Wario and how the universe came to be.
T he opposite of Mario is Wario, who is an idea if Mario was bad. He's tough and fast and like his greed for money!
T hen Mario is the opposite of what Wario is. He is clever and kind.
T he hero version of Wario
E at curry, gyoza and noodles, and spring rolls. I eat burgers, vegan, crunchy on the outside, soft in the middle with loads of cheese, mayonnaise, tomato, and one or two gherkins. I love the texture of pancakes and the sweetness of apples
R ecycling will change the world. I like clearing up a bit but not as much as making a mess

F red's my bro and likes all the things I like. I like playing games, watching TV, and snuggling up with him. I'd be lonely without him.

L ove dragons how they breathe fire. They are one of the most powerful and mythical creatures of time. I watched them at Chinese New Year in the city centre dancing and breathing fire.

Y es, there is Daddy, Mummy too, warm, cuddly, generous, and hard-working... I love you.

George Frank Gamble (8)

Boredom

I'm bored, I'm bored
I want to play
I'm bored, I'm bored
A game I say.

I'm bored, I'm bored
There's no one here
I'm bored, I'm bored
Am I going to be alone all year?

I'm bored, I'm bored
It isn't fair
I'm bored, I'm bored
I don't care.

I'm bored, I'm bored
I have nothing to do
I'm bored, I'm bored
I want to play a game or two!

I'm bored, I'm bored
There's no TV

I'm bored, I'm bored
You're so carefree.

I'm bored, I'm bored
It's only us
I'm bored, I'm bored
I should stop making a fuss.

I'm bored, I'm bored
It can't be true!
I'm bored, I'm bored
I'm alone with someone like you.

I'm bored, I'm bored
Go away
I'm bored, I'm bored
If you're not gonna play.

I'm bored, I'm bored
I've had enough!
I'm bored, I'm bored
Tough

Cos I am bored
And you are bored

Together, everybody's bored!

It isn't fair
We want a game
It isn't fair
You are so lame

Spirit of fun
Listen to us
We want something
Something fun

So everybody...
Speak now...
Everybody...
Play now...
Everybody...
Listen up...
Everybody...
Have fun!

Sumaya Omar (10)

This Is Me!

I would describe myself as many wonderful words
Maybe kind... maybe unique
But the word that most describes me is thoughtful
I love to be kind
I love to be brave
I love to be clever
But most of all I love to be thoughtful
And the way I am is because of the people who inspire me are
My mum because she is really helpful and I want to be helpful like her
My dad because he is brave and I want to be brave like him
My nana M because she is kind and I want to be kind like her
My grandad M because he is unique and I want to be unique like him
As you can see lots of people inspire me
Now I'm running late so I've got to go
Maybe see you another day
So far we'll
Goodbye.

Maya Rose Pugh (8)

Not One But Two

Hello, my name is Tyler
My life didn't have a good start
My mum didn't know how to raise me
So it was decided from her I should part.

I was put into foster care at eighteen months old
And a search began for a forever mum and dad
But for nearly two years no one came forward
This made me very sad.

Then one day two people came
They were friendly, funny and kind
"Hello I'm Simon", "Hello I'm Chris"
"We'd like to get to know you if you don't mind."

They visited me every day for over two weeks
Then suddenly I was living in their house
I was confused and very quiet
I couldn't speak, just squeak like a mouse.

They helped me and loved me
And I began to love them too

They bought me cool toys and we had so much fun
I said, "Can I stay forever with both of you?"

"Yes," they said and we went to see a judge
Who made it official and made me their son
And now as I grow they love me every day
Our family now has a dog and we have lots of fun.

I feel like the luckiest boy alive
Because I am not like my friends
I have not one but two amazing dads
Who I will love always until the end.

Tyler Forshaw-Abrahams (9)

I Am Me

I am me
I see myself smart,
I see myself with a big heart.
Many people tell me so,
I love to put on a show.
I desire a pet,
But my parents are still deciding so I shall not fret yet.
I enjoy reading, writing, watching, drawing and texting,
More things are acting, dancing, and don't forget to sing.
Being an author is amongst my dreams,
I like sewing mini cushions with perfect seams.
I love books and baking,
I will read pretty much anything.
Everyone loves my cookies,
I don't know how to swim but I'd love to learn and swim the seas.
Chocolate and cucumber are my favourite foods,
And my brothers are my favourite dudes.
I play netball - it's my favourite sport,

Do I play any other sport? No, nought.
Harry Potter is the best,
Followed by the Hunger Games and Noughts and Crosses and maybe in another poem, I'll tell you about the rest.
I hope you like me,
If you don't, I don't care because it means that you probably want to be me!

Rhea Chowdhury (10)

The Day That Silliness Came To Visit

The day that Silliness came to visit
They skipped down the street joyfully,
Playing fun and games together.
They ran up to the door, knocking on it.
Rushing away quickly, they hid,
Then popped up and said, "Boo!"
Then burst into laughter,
Their eyes beaming with joy, begging to have fun.
They wore bright, luminous clothes, beautifully shining.
One had a massive candy cane,
The other fidgeting with a yo-yo!
When I saw them I felt energised and excited
To have fun and be goofy with them.
We played 'The Floor is Lava'
Then went to KFC and ate together until the sun set.
We ate pizza and ice cream
And drank fizzy drinks like Fanta and Pepsi together.

They ate hungrily due to using lots of energy and playing often.
They also loved making faces out of their food.
They high-fived me and we cartwheeled,
Rolling like a ball down the street.
The next time Silliness comes we'll go and watch a movie together.
They remind me of my family.

Alfie Clark (10)

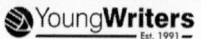

Tough Moments

I tremble through the hospital doors,
Knowing what's in my way,
Knowing it's the same war,
Between my feelings and my body,

My story's not the best,
And I don't know the rest,
It's not going great so far,
But for the future, I'll try my best,

When I was four it all went wrong,
Feelings inside me grew and grew,
I didn't want it to last for long,
But sadly it went on for many years,

I got older and older,
Until I fully understood, the deep truth,
Still, questions roam free through my head,
But I never manage to find answers,

Things happened that I could have never imagined,
I felt different, but not in a good way,

The other children would run and play,
And I would think, *why can't I be like them?*

There were ups and downs,
Until one day I thought to myself,
You only live one life,
Why let unfortunate things waste that precious time?

I try to constantly think positively,
Before all my immense hospital visits,
I cry, I laugh, I wonder,
But I will always appreciate who I am.

Clara Uddin (11)

Generations

With every generation
We have hope and creation...

Looking up at every dark, pollution-filled sky
We know we have a solution...

For every tree we knock down,
We plant and regrow
Making the air clean and free as we go...

For every living species
We make space and give them their own place, their own home...

With every can, bottle, paper we use
We can find ways to reuse...

For every hectic holiday, trip, or visit
It's only fair to share and go electric...

With every melting ice cap, the earth heating,
The seas rising, creatures disappearing...

Every generation
We can find better solutions through

Kindness and creation...

We need to stop being careless and
Raise awareness...

So, every generation
Let's make a promise...

We won't hide this in another folder
We will stand shoulder to shoulder

We won't cry and scream
We will fulfil our dreams

And we will show our worth
And rebuild this Earth

Every thoughtful action is just a fraction of
What we can do for the next generation.

Diya Purewal (9)

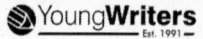

Anger Is Okay!

Anger lives deep inside everyone,
It's where our monsters hide,
Sometimes they like to burst out
Without us realising,
In case you didn't notice they like to come outside,
Anger likes to creep out
When the silliest things happen!
Like having to do something we don't like,
But it can also escape over bad things,
If you're called names or left out
Anger may seep out,
You should always ask someone for help
When your anger climbs out,
They might be able to help!
Anger can make you cry or kick or scream,
But that's okay!
As long as it is necessary,
And no one gets upset or angry
because then their monsters might fall out,
So one of the things to get your anger
To slide back down into the dark,

Is by simply having a hug
Or hearing some kind words,
Then I'm sure your anger will crawl down
Into the deep, dark place it emerged from
For a couple more days!

Aaliya Kaidi (10)

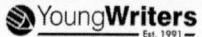

This Is Me Against Racism

When people judge me
Due to the colour of my skin,
It may not look like it hurts on the outside,
But it does hurt within.
Our skin should not be seen as a sin,
And if I could design a twin,
I would never tear off his skin
And throw it in the bin.
Sometimes we are insensitive
And say words that are offensive,
But remember a lost life is expensive.
Being bright is not just for the colour white.
All people should have the same right,
No matter your gender, race, or height.
So, let's make a change,
To make the world more inclusive and promise
To never be racially abusive.
It's stupid to judge someone
By the colour of their face,
Because we are all a part of the human race.
Let's educate ourselves together,

So that racism spreads never.
The world is full of humans,
Different in colour range.
We should cherish each other,
And never want them to change.

Troy Dennis (10)

Flowers Of Personality

Each and every plant has their own personality
And style, like us.
For example, you might have spiky hair...
No worries because a cactus is spiky too.
You may smell lovely; well lavender can relate.
Roses are beautiful don't you think?
Well so are you.
Most daisies are very tiny,
Some have maybe described you short/tiny
Just like these daisies.
Sunflowers are so bright just like the sun,
While you might smell like the fresh scent of mint.
Dahlias show elegance and dignity.
Some may describe you
As the symbolization for that flower.
Blue Iris symbolizes faith, hope, wisdom,
And purity.
If you're described this way, try showing curiosity.
Purple daisy; this shows innocence and loyalty,
Which you may show too.
(Also, it shows simplicity.)

The Bird Paradise shows love
And we all do that too.
(Also, it shows faithfulness and thoughtfulness.)
Geranium shows gentility
And you may do this too as well.

Mia Tongson (8)

My Tics Do Not Define

Imagine a funny feeling
An itch you cannot reach
Tics give me that feeling
It interrupts my speech

My face jerks and it twitches
My arm flies to the side
I scream and sometimes whistle
This makes me want to hide

These noises, they consume me
They take over my life
I just can't stop these tics
They cause me such a strife

Strangers can be rude to me
I just don't feel the same
Frowned upon and glared at
But I'm not the one to blame

My brain, it just misfires
Often doing its own thing

All-day long the tics are there
They're loud and exhausting

All I want is for inclusion
I'm just a normal kid
Don't judge me by my tics
It makes Mum flip her lid

My tics do not define me
Look past them and you'll see
Behind the noise and movements
I'm a girl who wishes to be free.

Lucy-Marie Phillips (11)

All About Me!

This is a poem all about me,
If you're quite interested
Then come along and you can see,
But if you're not just leave it be.

Wait,
You're here, you're interested,
So I'll tell you what I like to do,
Just give me a little space now
So I can start this poem for you.

I'm very, very confident in all that I do,
I like to bounce around like a baby kangaroo,
I bounce around the living room, falling over toys,
Laughing, laughing, laughing, making lots of noise.

I'm really good at gymnastics,
And doing lots of tricks,
I'm also good at singing,
And competition-winning,
And smelly rubbish binning,
And jewellery blinging.

But my very favourite dream...
Is acting,
Acting as princesses and queens,
Pirates who sail overseas,
And Alice at the Mad Hatter's teas
If I can make my dreams come true,
(Which I have),
So can you too!
And that's my poem... all about me,
I hope you enjoyed that,
Now buzz off like a bee.

Izzy Howe (9)

This Is Me!

This is me!
This poem that you're about to hear is sure to make you clap and cheer.
This poem that I'm about to write is sure to make you squeal in delight!
This poem will be all about me!
Like running fast, sport and climbing trees.
I like telling stories of the night that are sure to make you jump in fright.
I like spying and hiding in secret places.
I jump out at people, you should see their faces!
I like colouring and drawing and all that,
whereas my parents just like a good chat.
My brother Henry loves playing the drums and my grandma bakes cakes and lovely buns.
But this poem is not about them!
It's about me!
Yes me, the wonderful me
that loves climbing trees!

My favourite meal that I like to eat is Bolognese,
yum yum, what a treat.
I really hope you enjoyed this poem,
I'd love to stay but I really should be going.

Bethany Hood (9)

What Is Destiny?

Destiny is not your enemy
But it could be your fantasy
People say the best have it easy
But really no one can be the best
And this cannot be expressed enough
The best never gets to rest
They are always tested
What is destiny?
People say when you reach your destination
You're at peace but how can that be?
So, I bow down onto my knees
And I say what am I? What have I become?
Everyone knows we need trees to breathe
But then we cut them down
But I say we're all like trees
People try cutting us down but we stand tall
People can try to burn us but we can rise,
We are fire!
We can be whatever we want to be
But still what is destiny?
This is a question that is impossible to answer

But I'm possible,
We never know
What the future has planned for us!

Naima Murshida

This Is Me

A fool of a boy
So do not think that I am
A handsome person
A clever person
A compassionate person
I can always be a boy that is
Not handsome enough to have people look at me and say, "Hey Shiv, you are so handsome."
Not clever enough to even want to be a tremendous doctor
Not kind enough to buy presents for people that are close to me
I will never be
Having four fabulous sisters and a marvellous mum and dad
Loving Harry Potter
Going to school
I will always want to be
A dull discomfort to everybody that walks by me
A miserable, gloomy guy who is rubbish at everything
And rotting away in hell

A blood-curdling figure of mischief and disruption
I cannot be
Making magnificent Lego masterpieces
Reading eye-catching, remarkable books
Creative
I can never stop being
Me!

(Now read it from the bottom to the top!)

Shiv Dev (9)

Wish

I wish I didn't have to close my eyes to dream
I wish I could live the life ahead of me
I wish that no one chooses apart from me
I wish I, I wish I...

I want to be a wish come true
I want to be something new
Before I choose what wish to be
I will wish upon a star.

I wish I could move the mountains
I wish I could make the flames fly
I have to choose so I wish upon a star
I want to know which way to go
So I will wish from afar.

I wish that I could make the water into wine
I wish that I could make the world mine
I wish I, I wish I...
Keep wishing, you'll get there eventually
So I'll keep wishing and wishing
And wishing for me.

I wish I didn't have to close my eyes to dream
I wish I could live the life ahead of me
Wishing and wishing and wishing
It's how you get to where you want to be
So keep wishing.

Amelia Connolly (8)

This Is Me

Hi, I'm me and I'm full of glee,
I like to sing, and I love to swim,
I like to play games and I love to win,
(And so do you, but this is all about me!)
And I love to hear...
Birds singing peacefully,
And I love to watch...
Dogs eating greedily,
Yep, that's me!
My dream is to live in a mansion
With my dog so handsome.
I am fun and friendly,
Sometimes I worry but not to be sorry,
Because...
This is me and I am full of glee!
I feel free in my emotions,
I like to make funny potions,
From bottle lotions,
My sister makes me mad some of the time,
But when she's not making me mad,
She is making me glad.

By being fun and friendly
And always being there for me,
This is why I am making this poem to share.
Then I feel like that is fair.
And yes that is so much of me!

Lola Gardner (9)

The Two Contrasting Sides Of Me: Calm And Wild

Wild me:

I am like a caged bird,
I yearn to go out,

I sit in all day,
All day I pout,

I gaze out of the window,
At the pouring rain,

I can't go out,
To my heart this is pain,

Deep down in my heart,
I do nothing but mourn,

I put on my usual clothes,
All crisp yet worn,

I sit down to study,
And flip through my textbook,

As soon as I'm done, and let off the hook,

I will run wild,
Not in the slightest be mild,

No, I am lively, vivacious too,
I will not sit in any longer, and neither can you!

Calm me:

I must study,
And go to my dream school,

Not lounge around
In bed and drool,

With my tenacity, and willpower too,
I'll pass the exam with flying colours,

Even from the pedantic examiner's view,

Life has enjoyment, but study too,
I am working hard, just like you!

Arnav Ghoshal (10)

This Is Me

All of these skills and hobbies, where shall I start?
I focus and work hard at school,
Making me more smart,
I am learning French at home,
To talk to my best friend,
Whenever something goes wrong,
I make sure to amend.

I read and write to my heart's content,
Drawing and painting, so much time spent!
I write poetry too, acrostics and ones that rhyme,
Still reading when it's way past my bedtime.

I play football with my sister,
And read books to my little bro.
Trying to help people,
Even when they may be a foe,
I am confident and kind, well... most of the time!
And all the obstacles, I will be sure to climb.

I will be the best I can be!

Evelyn Edwards (11)

The Day That Silliness Came To Visit

Silliness came down the street,
Backflipping on horses
He peered through the window saying, "Hi"
His eyes were as white as a clown's wig
He wore a camouflage ninja outfit.

My eyes shone with joy when he came
We did knee-sliding challenges on the kitchen table
And upstairs we created a ninja obstacle course

We had a strawberry choc chip sandwich,
Washed down with grapefruit squash

When Silliness had to go he said, "See you soon, Racoon!"
I replied, "In a while Crocodile!"

The next time he comes round around
We will have founded a "Silliness Olympics"

He reminds me of my friends.

Ramin Ahmed (9)

Pretty Much All The Stuff About Me

My heart is on a race track,
My brain is meditating,
Life can be odd,
And sometimes irritating!

Never being bad,
Yeah, that's me,
Oh, except for that time,
I kicked someone in the knee.

I watch Mr Beast,
As a daily routine,
Then I have to go to school,
Even when I've broken my spleen.

Pizza is my favourite food,
I don't like anything more,
When I see it, I eat it,
Like a big, wild boar!

I stroke my cat Jerard,
Because he is so cute,
I played Fortnite,
And got some loot.

When I am angry,
I'll smash a TV,
And that is pretty much,
All the stuff about me!

Archie Wootton

This Is Hway

This is me,
I told Santa Claus I wanted real money for Christmas.
This is me,
I play hide-and-seek special edition
So when my brother finds me I tickle him.
This is me,
I'm special because I dared to ride down a tiger's throat that led me into the furious tiger's stomach.
This is me,
I took a bath with rose petals.
This is me,
I have so many clubs to go to.
This is me,
When I grow up I will build a new invention.
This is me,
I know how to use chopsticks.
This is me,
I have silky hair.

This is me,
When I was five I sent a rainbow drawing to the NHS.
This is me.

Hway Cheng (7)

This Is Me - My Day

My name is Nico
And I have brown hair.

I'm into Star Wars
And dinos here and there.

When my budgies escape,
I run downstairs,
Treading on Lego,
Without a care.

I get them to their cage
And I go to my room,
To listen to my music,
I like that bang and boom.

When it's time for school,
I act like a fool,
Make my friends laugh,
Play football.

When I get home, I'm feeling good,
So I go for a walk in my neighbourhood.

I see loads of trees
And some busy, buzzing bees,
I run, I shout,
I play about.

With my brother, I go back home,
It's time to end our really fun roam.

My tummy tells me it's time for dinner,
Pizza on the table - what a winner!

Nico Worswick-Hogwood (8)

A Recipe Of Kaitlyn

In a bowl add two large, mischievous eyes
Make sure they're not balls in disguise
Sprinkle in some smiling lips, mix well
It should form the shape of a shell.

Pour in two dancing feet
That shall be rather neat
Tip a cupful of waving hands
These will attract a lot of fans.

A cup of quietness would be nice
It can serve as a bit of spice
Add in some friendliness
Oh, and a pinch of mischievousness.

Spread a layer of wildness in
A bit of action, it shall begin
Perhaps a drop of craziness and a bake
Will not turn out as a big mistake.

Mix all the ingredients together
It should be as light as a feather
Fold and fry it carefully, then you will agree
This is me!

Kaitlyn Leung (10)

This Is Me

This is me!
I shall agree to help you
My favourite colour is blue
My name means fairy
I am always merry
I can be funny
I hate to spend a lot of money
I always try to make others happy
I don't be snappy
I try to make the world a better place
I think I really am an ace
I want to be an archaeologist
Some people want to be a biologist
I am very brave
I don't live in a cave
I'm not exaggerative
But I am very creative
I could cook a meal
I don't make it a big deal
I always bump my head
I hate to go to bed

I love to sing
How could I know what tomorrow will bring?
I'm eco-friendly
I'm also friendly
I love tea
So this is me!

Shofei Shanthakumar (9)

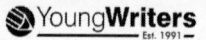

My Father

For me, he will always have care
The weight of my needs he will always bear
Whatever I need, with him I will always share
With me and the rest, he will always keep it fair.

He is like a cold shadow protecting me from the burning sun
And all the time he will give me moments of fun
Whatever I need doing he will always get it done
When I lost, he gave me hope and praised me lots when I won.

In the hardest times, he will cheer me up
Whenever I make a mistake, he will never be abrupt
When I need help, he will strengthen me harder
So how can I thank you my ever so beloved father?

Maheen Fahad (11)

This Is Me - Fred

My name is Fred
I like to go outside on an adventure to any place.
Cuddle my blanket.
Eat blueberry pie, hummus, mayonnaise, pizza, and yoghurt. Not all together though.
Watch Teen Titans Go, Sonic X and lots of others on Netflix and my daytime dream TV.
I like to run with Jess the dog.
Crash Bandicoot, Yoshi Island, Mario Maker and Sonic Advance 3.
Making crafts. All sorts.
Playing Lego, being creative
Cuddles from people that I like, like my brother.
My Toy Story mini-figures in my little wooden box.
I like to go outside best of all.
I like to cuddle the Earth.
I love the Earth. It tries to save itself.
I love nature.

Fred Gamble (7)

Two Words, About Me

I'm Scarlett,
Nickname Tinker.
10 years,
Creative thinker.

Crazy mum,
Playful dad.
Nottingham lass,
Yorkshire lad.

Two siblings,
Mason, T.
Silly brothers,
Annoying me.

Riding girl,
Love horses.
Trot, canter,
Over courses.

Two dogs
One's Stan.

Face hit
With pan.

Other one,
Name's Honey.
Loves having
Tickled tummy!

Have friends
Chloe, Dana
And Willow,
Silly bananas.

3 cats,
Bit aloof.
Catch mice
On roof.

Want to
Be vet.
Good grades,
Will get.

Brown hair,
Quite tall.
Green eyes,
That's all!

Scarlett Bartholomew (10)

My Funny Friend

You make me laugh
You dry my tears
And because of you, I have no fears

You're there for me when I need you
And for that I say thank you

You make me smile when I'm with you
You make me happy when I feel blue

Whether we're reciting the lines for our play
Or practising for our gym and dance display

Singing our carols is not hard to do
When I'm simply standing next to you

Sitting together is such a delight
We never put up a silly, small fight

When we are together, the world is just right.

Brooke Nicolette LoPinto

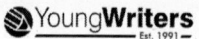

Teachings From My Memories

Memories, memories, they help me remember
All the things that happened last September
I fell off my bike and scraped my knee
And then it started to continuously bleed
I got back up with all my might
And soon forgot what happened that night
I only remember from the picture taken
When I cried as my knee was aching
Since that day I never looked back
Never ever had I been attacked
By the slander and gossip of other people
Nor the fear that seemed to ripple
Through my body
Or the neighbour's little doggy
My memories helped me to see
That perseverance is the key
Memories, memories are always there for me.

Hoda Ahmed (11)

My Pets

I'm a little bit like my fish -
I am quick in my movements.
I'm a little bit like my cat -
I am cuddly and friendly.
I'm a little bit like my dog -
I get over-excited when something good happens.
I'm a little bit like my chicken -
I like to explore the garden.
I'm a little bit like my monkey -
I'm good at baking.
I wish I had a chameleon, because
I change my mood a lot.
I am somewhat like my tiger -
I love to sprawl all over the carpet.
I don't quite think that I have anything in common with my tortoise...
Or my kangaroo.
Maybe I will get a panther next...

Isla Joliat (9)

The Girl In The Clouds

There was once a girl,
Who lived among the clouds.
Her dad's only rule,
Was to never wander beneath these clouds,
He told her stories of monsters beneath.

So, the cloud girl vowed,
To never wander beneath her clouds.
But one day,
Her dad turned his back.
So, she slipped underneath the clouds through
A tiny crack.

What she saw made her scream,
She hoped beyond hope,
That it was merely a dream.
And squeezed her eyes tight.
As tight as could be.

Luck was on her side this day,
For her dad came to take her away,

From the evil monsters that lurked below.
Humans.
As they were known.

Aisha Ali

Amazing Me!

O aka,
A mazing me!
K ind,
A rtistic.

R eading is fun!
O n the beam at gymnastics, I forward roll.
S wimming, stage 5, blue hat, I am.
E ggs I don't like you!

T o the tippy top of the climbing wall I go!
A rnan is my brother.
Y ellow and brown is my Brownie uniform.
L ook at the stories in my notebook!
O h, look my guinea pig Ginger is there!
R ound and round 1,000 times my hula hoop spins around my body!

Oaka Rose Taylor (7)

My Life In A Poem

In the morning my breath is as smelly as a baby's brown diaper.
When I finish dressing up I am as clean as the whitest thing you will ever see.
When I am on my way to school I am as moody as a black cloud.
When I come back from school I am as pleased as if it was the day I was born.
When it's time for dinner I am as hungry as a wolf searching for its prey.
When it's time for a snack I am annoyed just like lightning because there are no more snacks.
When it's time for bed I am elated as if it was my graduation in life.

Atiaat Bello

Reality Of Life

You see, when a big wave hits me,
I cannot see what waits ahead of me,
It trickles down my face like tears,
Like a spear, the coldness stabs my heart,
I do not want to part.

Life is like a reality show,
The Great British baker bakes her cake,
She is proud of her make,
But it drops off
In a big puff.

Life is like a board game,
You play to win,
But you end up like a lost pin.

I'm sad right now,
Because life isn't well,
Animals seek bad,
Loved ones hide, sad.

Amelie Raine (8)

I Love My Grandad

My grandad is a big, silly man,
He is one million thousand years old.
(That's a very big number)
He gives me sweeties when no one's looking,
He takes me to the golf course
To throw meatballs for the dogs.
He lets me go in the front of the car,
He's a very cheeky man.
He always wears the same black jumper.
We sit together and watch 'Break The Wall',
And we even cook Spanish tortilla.
I love my grandad,
I love him so much.
He's as shiny as a shoe polish
And that is that.

Ralph Mahadevan (3)

How To Make A Friend Like Me!

First, put in a bucketful of love to warm up your heart
Secondly, add a cup of happiness and laughter to make long-lasting memories
Afterwards, add a dash of playfulness and lots of fun times
Next, sprinkle some generosity in the mixture to spread kindness
Then add a spoonful of cleverness to help all of those all around you
After that, pour in a drop of craziness so every day is exciting
Finally, add a splash of creativity to brighten up your day
Remember to be thoughtful, caring and sweet then you will have a friend like me.

Isabelle Evans (8)

This Is Me

I'm only ten,
And my dreams are as tall as Big Ben.
I want to be a fashion designer but also a vet.
I am great in English but not so good in maths,
I'm passionate about art and I love to have a blast.
I'm always smiling and very prepared,
When my teacher forgets something
I'm always there.
My favourite colour is violet and I like lilac,
I love to paint and I have a favourite saint.
I have two pups and I love to say, "'Sup!"
My fears are clowns when they dance all around,
My strength is designing gowns.
This is me!

Sofia Dantas (10)

I Am Me!

I have a difficult name,
Which can be a challenging game,
My mum thinks I'm quite hyper
Just because I broke her best jar.

I've always loved 'How to Train Your Dragon'
But my mum thinks they are horses with wagons,
You might think I'm mean
Like a rotten bean.

I like football
Even though I'm not tall,
I can hear my name being called
Because I'm cool.

When I'm older I want to rule
Not the world but an amazing school,
I'm going to be better at football
And hear more of my name being called
Because, remember, I'm cool!

Juwayriyah Noor (9)

The Power Of My Identity

Conquering the world with the power I got,
This talent took me a while to spot.
Never learnt to look back,
I am always on my track.
This power is so unique,
I have always aimed for an ambitious peak.
People can't judge me with their own thoughts,
I am telling you why because those people
Never had good minds like you lot.
Jealousy is not in my blood,
If you challenge me
I will attack you like a flash flood.
You will never be able to stop
This strength from spreading,
You will find out why
Just sneak through the heading.

Utkarsh Gupta (11)

This Is Louisa

Hi, my name's Louisa,
I'm as happy as can be.
I am 8 years old,
Which means I'm in Year 3.

I have a brother and a sister,
Mum and dad too.
We all live in Edgware,
How about you?

My face is full of freckles,
My eyes are bright blue.
I may be quite little,
But there's nothing I can't do.

Dancing, singing, drawing -
They're my favourite things to do.
I love to go swimming,
And play with my friends too.

I hope you enjoyed my poem
And discovered something new.
There's only one me -
Now tell me about you!

Louisa Schock (8)

I Am Kira

Unicorns, mermaids, rainbows, snow,
hearts and sweets I like them so.
Penguins, rabbits, pandas too...
all so cute just like you.
Ice cream is so yummy,
choco cookies in my tummy.
Tomatoes are so round and red,
but I don't like them fed.
Bears and witches are both so scary,
I'd rather see a nice little fairy.
My teddies and art,
are in my heart.
Dancing to the music, dressed in pink and blue,
using glitter and glue.
Mango and lychee,
are tasty for me.

Kira Pau (8)

Who Am I?

My favourite things are
Happiness and friendship
For they are invaluable
They can help you go on
Friends are there to help you
But you must do the same.

It is my dream to become a footballer
And if I don't get it
I won't be disheartened
For there is always a second chance
If you give up, what will you get
So always go on and have determination.

Don't hurt people because they'll hurt you back
Instead, be kind and watch how they help you
And then you'll realize it is better to be kind
That is how I make friends.

Parshva Mehta (8)

I Dream

I dreamt that the world went black
And the sky cried with rancid rain
Next in line, my humble house
Crumbled down
The sand on the beach was rotten grain.
I dreamt that the sky went blue
And the hills blossomed glowing flowers
The birds shaped a heart
And in the sky
The glistening sun shone for hours and hours.
I dreamt that the trees could walk
And the flowers could talk in whispers
The grass you could eat in a pudding pie
And I had one hundred smiling sisters.

Memphis Morris (10)

I Am...

I am brave, I am fearless, I am strong, this is me
I can survive tarantula twists and tornado turns
I am passionate about all things fun
And all things funny.

This is me, this is creative me
I am messy I am colourful
I can craft and paint.

This is me, this is fit me
I can run, I can swim
I can dribble a football.

This is me, this is musical me
I can play delightful music
I can play the piano
If I believe in myself.

I am brave, I am fearless, I am strong, this is me
I can survive tarantula twists and tornado turns.

Daniel Houghton (8)

I Am...

I am brighter than the sun
More funny than funny fun
More smiley than a grinning face
More beautiful than white silk lace
More honest than when you said about that ruler that you kept
More happy than a dancing bride
More proud than the greatest pride
More swift than a silver sword
More precious than a gold award
More cosy than a cosy nook
More loved than the greatest book
But I'm really not as good as you
With the person you are and the things you do.

Molly Kennedy (9)

Be The Best I Can Be

Football is the best put me to the test,
Be the best I can be.
My aim of the game is to win the match,
Be the best I can be.
I want to reach the stars as high as Mars,
Be the best I can be.
Alert, alert, time to work,
Be the best I can be.
English, maths and history,
Geography is a mystery
Be the best I can be.
I have some fears,
But mostly ideas,
Be the best I can be.

I need to understand the grand journey of life,
So that I can be the best I can be.
So as you can see
This is me,
Being the best I can be.

Beatrice Clark

Ode To Rocky

What makes me happy and what makes me, me?
Well, that is easy,
It is my dog Rockeeee,
He is lovely, loving and kind,
When I want a cuddle, he just seems to read my mind.

But not just him, all dogs have that magic,
To see what you need to them is simply automatic,
Often they bark
'Specially when it is time to go to the park.

Dogs are amazing in so many ways
Obedient and loyal, all of their days,
Great Danes, Chihuahuas, Labradors and Dachshunds too,
No matter what they are they will always love you.

Isla Foden-Reekie (9)

This Is Me

Have you ever
Bullied someone
Or been unkind?
So entwined you
Don't realise
You could be categorised
You wouldn't want
That would you?
Have you ever thought
How they felt?
Just watched their heart
Slowly melt into where no light shines
You can hear their cries
Let's be kind
And take a rewind
Can you ever find
The kind from deep within
Then you can start to begin
To understand your actions
Are a sin.

Marina Rutherford

My Identity

My identity is linked to a land littered with castles,
Untold stories and the promise of
great things to come.
My identity is not defined by my skin colour
Or whether I was born in the sweetest valley
Or the hustling and bustling city.
My identity celebrates my uniqueness
Whether I speak the language of Heaven or not.
My identity inspires passion, pride
Whenever I sing Hen Wlad Fy Nhadau
And shout,
"Cymru/Wales! Cymru/Wales! Cymru/Wales!"

Seren Bowen

This Is Me

Courageous, intelligent, friendly, creative
Courage is a part of me, taking part in everything,
I am intelligent and super smart,
My fun, imaginative mind
These are some qualities that make me
This is who I am meant to be,
This is me,
Everyone solves problems
But it matters how you do it
Everyone is different
Unique and beautiful in their own way
And this is the best version of what you can be
This is the best version of me
This is me!

Angelina Dhir (11)

This Is Me

"This is me,"
Said Amy one day,
"I've got green eyes
I hate flies
And my favourite colour is grey."

"This is me,"
Said Sam one night,
"I've got black skin,
I love to sing,
And darkness gives me a fright."

"This is me,"
Said Elliot one afternoon,
"I've got blond hair,
I like to share,
And I hate the colour maroon."

"This is me,"
I said one morning,
"I love poems,
They keep me going,
And I enjoy drawing!"

Felicity Payton (10)

This Is Me!

B ravery is my heart
E nergy is my soul
T alented in my brain
H appiness in my smile
L ove in my spirit
E ducation in my conscience
H elpfulness in my country
E motion on my face
M atureness in me

This is me
My name is Bethlehem
I am 9 years old
My hobby is skateboarding
My favourite food is burgers
I am in Year 5
My favourite subject is maths
This is me!

Bethlehem Bereket (9)

The Life Of Me

I am an 8-year-old boy
I like Lego toys
I speak some jokes
To tickle my folks.

I'm the middle child
My younger brother is wild
Me and my sister always fight
Because she thinks she's always right.

I am skilful
When playing football
Man United is my team
To play for them is my dream.

I am as quick as a flash
And love to spend cash
Coins have left my sack
So I've made a shop to get money back.

I am an intense gamer
Some say I'm an aimer
Veg is my thing
It helps me to win.

Musa Chowdhury (8)

But That's Just Me!

My life is fairly bland,
But that's just me!
I may not be rich
But that's just me!
When I wake up in the morning
I brush my teeth
And that's just me!
You may not know my favourite colour is blue
But maybe not for you
But that's just me!
We are all different which is completely fine!
You can love something
And I can love something else
I like spelling
And that's just me!
And this poem is all about…
Me!
And also I like sleeping in the dark
But that's just fairly me!

Luqman Lockwood (9)

This Is Me

I have hair as black as the midnight sky
The tint of a raven in my eye
My skin as smooth as silk
My teeth as white as milk

But does this really matter?
Is it only looks that flatter?
It should be the personality that counts
As this can come in big amounts

Inside, my heart means well
"I want to make a difference," it tells
My intentions are only good
When will this ever be understood?

Everyone has a heart
They just need to see
That everyone has two sides
And that this is me.

Nikita Padki

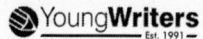

How To Bake A Cringy Cake

Cringiness
Rice
Ice
No sugar, milk or eggs
Grapes
Honey
Yoghurt
Cool water
Apple slices
Cocoa powder
Vegetables

Method:
First, put rice in a bowl and put in ice and cool water
Then hide grapes and apple slices in the ice
After that, put on some honey and yoghurt
Sprinkle some vegetables around it

And sprinkle cocoa powder
Add some cringiness
You are down with your cringy cake - enjoy!

Lana Reza (8)

Messi The Man

M essi the man does what he can
E very game he is energetic and athletic
S even years old he was scoring goals
S eeing him in the Hall of Fame
I nspiring me to represent my country

T he beautiful game
H elps join the population
E xciting atmosphere all round

M essi the man, the man for assists
A t Camp Nou he breaks the records
N o one can beat him for now...

Leo Assad (9)

Busy!

This is me
Ding, ding, ding
My alarm clock rings
For me a happy sound
I really don't like sitting around.

This is me
School is next
No time to rest
I am so excited for lunch break
I really hope the pudding is cake.

This is me
Home I go
The awful traffic is so slow
Now I have an exhausted mind
I feel I am ready for glorious bedtime.

This is me
The weekend arrives again
There's nothing now to complain
My friends are on the way
I really hope we can do some role-play.

Ella Brophy (9)

I Love Coding

I love coding
But not just pulling information
Keeping the computer cool,
So it doesn't stall,
Sit up there for an hour a day,
Although I would stay
For hours if I had my way,
Coding Docker is more challenging
Than Python or Scratch,
So I must hatch a plan,
So it doesn't corrupt or interrupt my SD card,
It's so hard,
But the thrill of the project
Drives me forward to the end,
Let's start again!

Oliver King (11)

Being 11!

Paddleboarding, climbing, Scouts and fishing too,
These are all the things I enjoy,
Why don't you join in too?

I'd rather be out than stuck indoors,
Riding my bike, making dens, exploring the woods
Playing with friends.

Come rain or snow, in shorts I'll be,
Playing and running happily.

Camping is a favourite,
Along with swimming in the sea,
Climbing mountains and reaching goals,
This is me!

Ethan Parker (11)

This Is Me

I am a...

Dashing defender
Sausage lover
Maths genius
Epic gamer
Red ring head
Cool cat
Creamy substance hater

  T he dashing defender
  H ating anything creamy
  I am as cool as a panda
  S ausage and chips are the best

  I nterlocking red rings on my head
  S illy family

  M aths is the number one subject
  E yes are an endless sea of blue.

Otto Cheffers Gibbs (10)

This Is Me

Outside I am happy
On the inside I'm lonely
A few friends to keep me company

It makes me happy
I have tried and tried and tried
It makes me scared
To make a friend

When I open my mouth to speak
All it does is make me freak
I try but struggle
It's like a long dark tunnel

If you want to be friends with me
I would probably jump with glee

This is me, this is my social anxiety.

Bethan Everett (11)

My Anger And Sadness

It's stuck inside my body.
You can let it out by talking to someone.
You can't shut the door and walk away!

Talk to the heart, but not the face.
Eating crisps all alone, you can't even taste them...
Not even my favourite type.

Horses and knights try to distract my brain.
My eyes are swelling all backwards.
But then I learn this is all part of life.
I must learn to deal with all troubles and strife.

Paige Lewis (8)

This Is Me!

I am as funny as a clown,
I am as messy as a monkey.
I am fun like a playground,
I am as exciting as a fair.
I am as thankful as a nurse,
I am as thoughtful as a caring vet.
I am as caring as a doctor,
I am as smiley as a saint.
I am as happy as a mouse that has cheese.
I am as creative as an artist,
I am as helpful as a sidekick.
I am Alma.
I would like to be a vet when I'm older.
This is me!

Alma Miles Herrera (7)

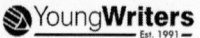

Who Am I?

Open your eye, let me know, who am I?
Keep others mad because I'm glad.
I'm above in studies, having many buddies,
I always rule because I'm cool,
I feed the needy, hate the greedy,
Like multiplication and addition,
Not subtraction and division,
Master in times tables but not eating vegetables,
I always share, but nobody cares,
So feeling sad, I'm not bad,
Poor in football but love it all.

Muhammad Ahmed Khan (9)

This Is Me

I love animals, they are so cute,
Strawberries are my favourite fruit.
My cat is orange and fluffy,
But my dogs are rather scruffy.
I love and adore tigers,
Also, I love baby ligers.
I am respectful, loving and kind,
And I also have a great mind.
My favourite colours are purple and pink,
I love school but it makes me overthink!
My favourite subject is art,
And I think I have a great heart.
Connie and Matilda are my best friends,
And now this poem ends.

Jasmine Mayne (8)

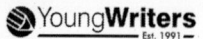

Our Wellbeing

Love lives in the heart,
Where family and friends stay.

Anger stays in the hand,
But tries not to come out.

Tears live in our eyes,
But will always come out with joy
Or sadness.

Sometimes we might get hurt,
But our features in our body
Are here to protect us.

I have hands, legs and many more,
But I don't use them for hitting or biting.

Reneika White (10)

The Kindness River

Kindness should be flooded
No one should be excluded.
Always treat people equally
Let people sleep peacefully.

It doesn't cost anything
But it means everything.
Even if it is a stranger
You can be a life-changer.

A little more kindness
Say, "No more selfishness!"
Spread kindness on the street
Even behind the screen.

Kindness is needed more
We must make it better than before.
We need to do this together
This should happen forever!

Thiviya Kamalendran (10)

My Fantastic And Wonderful Adventure

I found a balloon,
It was the shape of a baboon,
The trees waved at me,
As a bee flew by me,
I found an odd-looking key,
It had some sort of guarantee,
I trotted across the grass,
As I pumped a great big gas,
My belly rumbled,
As my friend tumbled,
I picked up a flower,
As my friend poured some flour,
I left the park with a great big stomp,
As I fell and grew a great big bump.

Simar Kaur (7)

This Is Me

I am silly
I've got friends
Including Millie.

I adore my cats
Cats called Roo and Coo
We got them a mat
For their chairs a week ago too
Roo is big
And Coo is mini.

I, well, I am kind
I am loving
And have an open mind
And this is the kind of thing I am...

...Sometimes bad
Sometimes good
Or maybe mad...

Best of all is my kindness.

Poppy Sandamas (8)

This Is Me

I wish I was good at starting a rhyme
I wish I could go to bed on time

I wish that I was tall
But I am really small

I wish that I was louder
And maybe a little prouder

I wish I didn't have a scar
And I could run really far

I suppose at least I've written this
And it's fun giving bed a miss

My taller friends look after me
And my scar shows my history

I will never be good at running
But you can't have everything.

Holly Bannister (11)

Being Me

Who am I?
Sometimes I'm a bird in the sky,
Or a leaf on a tree,
In front of new people a little bit shy,
I'm anything I want to be...
Head in the clouds,
Feet on the ground,
Sometimes feel upside-down,
Can't sit still, like to travel around,
Running feet, happy head...
Leaving the rest,
Just doing my best...
Until the day is done and it's time for bed.

Anu Sathya Umashankar (10)

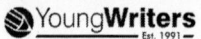

My Recipe

How you make a Chloë!
Open 3 tins of baking
Add Willow and other friends
Two cups of out of the ordinary
600g of design and make
Stir in some art
Add 12 cups of kindness
And 5 cups of energy
Add 40g of creativity and fun
And 3 cups of hungriness
Plus 1 1/2 cups of obedience
1kg of love for rabbits
And finally, 5 cups of eagerness
And you now have a Chloë!

Chloë Alexander (10)

Me And FNAF

M ay I mention I'm the best, better than all the rest.
E ggs are gross, along with ham, all should be burnt in a pan.

F un to fill spare time
N ever gets boring, but Fortnite does.
A great way to have lots of fun, and that's why I write this as it is a buzz.
F NAF is best, better than the rest, so when you see some other games you think of them as less.

Louis Roberts (10)

Ozzy The Octopus

O zzy is incredible and so lively
C onnor is his best friend, they make up the Ozzy Swirl
T ogether him and Ozzy are a team always
O zzy has lots of friends, they met at the underwater Olympics
P ut food a mile away from him and he will run as fast as he can
U seless Uma is Ozzy's worst enemy
S ome say the underwater Olympics isn't a thing but it is.

Brody Lineham (10)

This Is Hanaa

This is me,
I am me,
Me is Hanaa,
And Hanaa is me.

I love a lot of foods
As it puts me in a good mood,
As well as my brother who has just moved.

At school, I like to play
With my friends,
Throughout the day.

When I get home, I watch TV
To watch my favourite Disney movie.

My favourite animal is black and white,
Which has lots of fur,
To keep warm in the night.

Its name is Panda
And my name is Hanaa
Hanaa is me,
And I am me!

Hanaa Rashid (7)

My Mum

Thank you for everything
You have a loving heart
When you go out all the birds start to sing
My taste buds are joyful
When I have your cherry tart
I fall apart when you're not around
You are the most caring
You remind me of a tree
And you are very sharing
Because without you, I can't breathe
You make me feel safe
You're the reason that I make my bed every day!

Malayka Moeed Yazdani (9)

All About Me

A leena is my sister
L oser means my brother
L aiba is my name

A n artist I became
B ig ideas, small creations
O nly my brother wants a PlayStation
U nder here, over there
T here are hypotheses everywhere

M any people say I'm crafty
E choes whisper inside my head, I think it's time to go to bed!

Laiba Syed (10)

This Is Me

I like reading
I love to write
Books keep me up
Late into the night.

Cricket is good
I'm best with a bat
Horseriding's fun
With boots and a hat.

I have three rabbits
They're miniature lops
They chew up the carpet
And they hop, and they hop.

Going to Belgium
Was my favourite trip
With chocolate waffles
And mayo and chips.

I like the ocean
It's calming blue.
Being in water is great.
How about you?

Rose Tappin (10)

All About Me

I was born on the second of September,
I like reading and I want to be a vet,
Once a dog barked at me
And thought my scooter a threat!
I like having fun with numbers,
And in my school, you have to wear jumpers!
In our school, to help us, we have rules,
And that is cool,
Unless you are a fool.
On Saturday to classes I go,
They are ballet and taekwondo!
My favourite sport is swimming,
And I like having fun singing.

Ruth George (8)

This Is Me!

I played the toot,
Now I am on the flute.
This is me and I am free.

Frightened of aeroplanes,
Izzy is my name.
This is me and I am free.

I love reading,
I would never dream of stealing.
This is me and I am free.

Netball is for me,
Especially the match teas.
This is me and I am free.

Timid and shy,
But learning to fly.
This is me and I am free.

But most importantly,
I love my family.
This is me and I am free.

Isabelle Clarke (10)

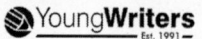

All About Myself!

When it is night, I feel like a fight
Which is my right
When I see the moon,
I start to hear the melody tune
As soon as it's morning, in comes the light
Then I say, "Let's fly a kite!"
No one can be like me,
Since I'm always free
At hometime, I stand in the hut,
With my mouth shut
I really want a chocolate bar,
Sitting in my small car.

Santosh Tal (9)

The Great Outdoors

Tumbling through a meadow,
Tears of laughter at my eyes,
Dressing up as fairies,
Levelling my lows and highs.

Gliding through a lake,
Around me flows the purest calm.
Underneath me in the clear, cool land,
Creatures gently glide, free of alarm.

This is the great outdoors,
Life has never been so much fun,
The bestest friend I could ever have,
Underneath that blazing sun.

I love the great outdoors!

Genevieve Jefferys (10)

My Cat Coco Be Like

One
Two
Three
Crash!
Oops
Wasn't my fault.

Four
Five
Six
Boom!
Oops
Wasn't my fault.

Coco will pounce any second, any minute
You can never dodge
Move
Wiggle
Nudge
Or neither budge.

Seven
Eight

Nine
Zoom!
Oops
Wasn't my fault.

Ruhaniya Khalid (8)

The Meaning Of My Name

L istening to Michael Jackson
I like to watch The Masked Singer
T heatre club is where I shine like a star
T o strum on my guitar
L ego ignites my imagination
E mmy is my favourite dog

F amily time is fun
I enjoy playing on my switch
R ainbow High is my most colourful toy
E nya, this is me!

Enya Smith (8)

Flexible Me

Twirling, swirling, hopping about,
Laughing and smiling, I'll give you a shout

Cartwheeling and backbends all around,
I can't sit still, I'm always making a sound

Dancing and jumping is what I do best,
Come and join me in this fun fest

You'll never be bored when you're with me,
Let's get together, as I'm great company!

Safa Hussain (8)

The Unknown

In all the kids in my school
I may not be the tallest
Of all the voices in the world
Mine may be the smallest
And out of all the runners in the country
I could be the slowest
But
Out of all my town
My heart is the largest
Out of all the kids in my school
I shall be the kindest
All the people in the world
Think my art is the coolest
And every creature in the universe
Noticed my dreams are the biggest.

Mia King (11)

All About Khatijah

K ind and not that funny
H ates school Mondays
A nd loves school Fridays
T op of all food - mint choc chip ice cream
I have a kitten soo fluffy and cute
J am on bread, nice but not that good
A house I'm still moving into
H ow I just love school

K ind, my friends say but I don't believe them.

Khatijah Khan (9)

Finlay's Poem

I am kind and caring
I am honest and truthful
I am a cheetah running across to the distance
I have a lion's bravery
I have the memory of an elephant
I am great at sport
I am best at gaming
I am great at helping and making friends
I can show respect to others
I can find school easy
I can find school a challenge
I have the skills of an actor
I am a dolphin swimming across the sea
This is me!

Finlay Hudd (11)

My Day

T eacups empty in the morning,
H appy on the way to school,
I play with my friends
S itting on my chair in class,

I happily eat my snack,
S itting on the dining table, eating my lunch, munch, munch, munch,

M y mum is waiting for me to take me to the mosque
E very day, nonstop, it makes me, me!

Talha Patel (7)

This Is Me

I'm always bouncing about
I have a bright smile
I'm never sad or grumpy,
It's always nice to be me,
It's very easy to spread,
Without me, you wouldn't have fun,
You'll feel me when you get a medal.
If your friends cheer you up you will feel this emotion
You'll feel this feeling when you get a present
What emotion am I?

Annousheh Sayed (8)

All About Me

How the sun shines
The one thing that makes me smile
During my sad times
I am happy during the day
But sad at night
Oh, how the sun shines
Chocolate, art, rocks, and leaves
Pour down the drain as the rain goes away
Drip-drop on the dustbin
As I sit there in the window
My fist under my chin
Outside it's grey
Inside me is grey.

Sara Szymaniak (11)

Bored

Supposing you were bored,
The chores were all chored.
What would you do?
What could you do?
If it was too rainy to play,
On this damp autumn day.
What would you do?
What should you do?
Well, you could write like a poet,
Climb up the tree so it,
Would seem to throw away the time,
Because sometimes,
You may be bored,
But trust me I'm sure,
There are always things to do, all around you.

Madeline Merritt (10)

I Am Alice

A lice
L ovable and caring
I ce cream is my favourite
C lever at school
E verywhere

R unning around the tennis court
O r dancing on stage
W hatever the weather I try and try
L ike having sleepovers with my friends
E njoying my life
Y es, it's great to be me!

Alice Rowley (8)

I Like...

I like stationery,
The ones that smell like...
Chocolate and ice cream,
Those I'll never sell.

I like making,
Arts and crafts,
Building stuff,
Making mini rafts.

I like eating,
Mac and cheese,
It makes me smile,
I want more, please.

I like squishes,
Big or small,
Whatever size,
I love them all.

I like tortoises,
They walk so slow,
I asked my mum to get one,
But she said no.

Mia Opoku Agyeman (9)

This Is Me

I am as fearless as an eagle
As curious as an inquisitive kitten
I am like a candle
Which burns itself to give light to others
Not able to illuminate everything
But always more than enough
If I were part of the solar system
I would be the sun
Rising above in the sky
Shining with pride
Giving light to all
No matter who is who.

Haleema Zeeshan (11)

My Dream Comes True

When I grow up,
I want to be a footballer away from home.
When I grow up,
I want to be the best footballer.
I will try at school to see if I can be the best,
They said I have to wait until I'm older,
So I said, "Okay."
A few years later, they were training,
And the manager was on his phone,
He said I can be a footballer.

Jayden Rowlands (9)

This Is Me

This is me, I have two cats
One is thin and one is fat
Both of them have lots of fluff
And they like to think they're tough.

This is me, I have a brother
And a father and a mother,
I like to play computer games
While Daddy goes and flies a plane.

This is me, I play the drums
Trying not to hit my thumbs
Mathematics is my favourite class
And playing football on the grass.

Ezekiel Han (9)

This Is Me

I am funny, I like quizzes
A fan of cats
With hair as black as a night owl
This is me

I am a diamond saviour, I am a fan of snowmobiles
A hater of bullies
With a frown as big as a Bently
This is me

I am nice, I am strong
A friend of honest and delighted friends
With a big smile like an ocean wave
This is me.

Ilyas Connelly (9)

What A Life!

What a life
Living in fear, sorrow, and vexation
Scared and unhappy
What a life!
Feeling tormented and agitated
Having terrifying feelings
What a life!
Working hard to get out of this situation
But I just can't
What a life!
Feeling frustrated and rejected
Feeling weak and ashamed
What a life!
Been stranded and tired
What a life!
I'll never wish to live such a life.

Amanda Dike (12)

This Is Me!

I am friendly like a happy bee
My favourite lesson is PE
Pizza is my favourite food
It puts me in a super mood
I love my family to the moon
Their love would maybe fill a room
I love playing Roblox when I can
I played it at Jake's in a gaming van!
Now I'm sure you can tell and I'm sure you can see,
That this awesome poem is all about me!

Ashley Cunningham (8)

Me

I love my family, and also my friends,
I don't think that it will ever end.
We don't have a big house,
But we live next to the sea,
But life is best with my family and me.
I like playing football, scoring many goals,
I'm so grateful that I am not living in the cold.
I try to save the world, for there is no Planet B,
But life is best with my family and me.

Luke Laloux (9)

This Is Me

My favourite animal is a panda
Because they are really cute!
I enjoy doing cooking with my mom
Especially cookies.
I enjoy exploring the garden
And watching the ants marching, 1, 2, 3.
I like watching for butterflies and birds.
I love going to the park
With my bicycle and ringing the bell
With a *ting-a-ling-ling!*

Anisah Haseeb (8)

All About Me

My name is Layan
I like cats but I don't like bats
I am funny and I always like bunnies
So furry and cute they are loved and liked
Watermelons are my favourite fruit
Pomegranates are my second
And I reckon the strawberries are my third
I am a girl
I like ice cream and I am so kind
This is me
So let it be
This is me so funny and kind
And that is who I am.

Layan El-Wakhery (10)

This Is Me!

F un game whether you win or lose.
O bviously, we never get to choose!
O ur football fans are there to cheer.
T hey love the game, so they won't fear!
B eing brave and following your dream
A nd keeping it real, while they all scream!
L etting people know who they like
L oudly, sending messages while I strike!

Saim Yasir (10)

Ruby's Poem

I am Ruby
I am nine years old
I am tall
I am brave
I am clumsy
I am funny
But I am still Ruby
I am loud
I am kind
I am caring
I am fierce
I am beautiful
But I am still Ruby
I get sad
I get angry
I get happy
I get over-excited
I get shy
But I am still Ruby

I am me.
And me is all of these put together.
Ruby is just perfect in every little way.

Ruby Mae Dignam (9)

This Is Kayla

My name is Kayla, I'm very cool,
Sometimes I fancy playing a bit of pool.
I am kind and I will help you out if you're in a bind.
I like to sing, dance and braid my hair,
And when it comes to friends, I really care.
I giggle, laugh and play a lot,
And when it comes to exercise I like to squat.
Now you know that this is me,
I think I fancy a cup of tea!

Kayla Ovadia

Just Me

I'm me,
And no one will change that.
Just me.

I can be happy or joyful,
Cross or angry.
Sad or confused,
But that's just me.

I have talents,
I have inabilities.
I have failures and successes,
That's just me.

My dream is to be a poet,
To write books and stories.
A dream of mine,
A dream for me.

I'm me,
And no one will change that.
Just me!

Mila Patel (9)

My Football Dream

When I grow up I want to be inspirational,
Tell everyone facts and be educational,
I want to be a woman's football player,
Be kind and be a rule obeyer.

I will kick the ball like a boss.
Never letting my team suffer a loss,
I will use my tactical skills,
And pay the bills.

I will be the best I can be!

Cadence Edwards (8)

I Exist By My Choices

I have a little world in my life
My dreams sometimes take flight
I can't find a way out heaps of times
At times like this
I remember my choices
All of them are my voices
Of course, I can make mistakes
Or I can find the right way in places
Under any circumstances;
I get rid of all the destroyers
Because I exist by my choices
All of them are my voices.

Gulcihan Cakir (9)

Angry

When the red mist is swirling,
The tornados are curling.

With thunder booming and lightning striking,
There really isn't a more terrifying sight.

The bright wildfires licked the trees,
But at night the earthquakes demolish the cities.

And the whirlpools are gushing,
The tsunamis are rushing.

When the volcanos are erupting,
Then anger is boiling.

Felix Pace (9)

All About Me!

T alking and talking is what I do.
H appy smiles are what I wear.
I ce cream is my favourite treat.
S unny days, I like the heat.

I nteresting thoughts are in my head.
S hort naps in my bed.

M ilkshakes are what I drink.
E nding this poem will make me sink.

Abdullah Binn-Omar (10)

This Is Me, Iris

T wo favourite animals - tigers, dolphins.
H appy as a tiger cub
I love tiger cubs
S weet as a candy cane.

I love dolphins
S hiny as a pearl.

M y tiger and dolphin
E asy to love.

I love tiger cubs
R oar!
I love tigers and dolphins
S ee them for yourself.

Iris Perry (9)

I Am Cool

I am cool,
I like to go in the pool.
I like food,
But mushrooms are rude.
I like looking at the TV screen,
But when I play games, it makes me scream!
I like to go on my iPad,
But when Mum says no, it makes me sad.
I like McDonald's, they give me chips,
But the salt tingles on my lips.

Lucas Seager (7)

We Are Unique

I might be taller,
I might be older,
I might be blonde,
I know the clothes I wear are different,
I know I may be different from you,
I may think different,
I may act different,
But we know,
Although I'm me,
And you are you,
I know we're all unique,
But that doesn't mean we can't all do one thing,
Be kind.

Casey Smith

My Perfect Day

With birds in the sky, people gleaming with smiles.
Children eating sweets with faces full of joy.
The sun shining brighter than it ever has.
Green grass moving about in the warm air.
People pick flowers and ride bikes.
A day filled with fun swimming and picnic times.
When the light went out, started the day again.

Joey Baker (11)

Me And Her

This is me, and
This is her
Same soul,
Different shapes
I share milk...
She shares toys
I share love...
She shares games
She is mine, and
I'm hers
And together...
Share a heart
The same mum and the same dad
Brother and sister
Kevin and Ella.

Kevin Monu (8)

My Favourite People

My favourite people are
Mummy and
My daddy and
My cousins and
My aunties and
My grandma,
I admire all these people
Because they are my family and they are nice,
They do jigsaws with me
And I love watching TV with them.
I love them all because I am so small.

Ishaal Liaqat (6)

Bernice

B eginning to be better
E ager to learn
R eady and steady
N ever going to give up
I ncredible, smart
C ool and respectful
E xotic and kind.
All of these are the traits I have because
I'm unique and nobody's like me!

Bernice Ndu Ariolu

My Family And Me

Every day and week
Turns into every month and year
Maths and English I like
I also ride a bike
I'm the oldest child
Though I'm not that mild
Drawing is where I'm good
I like running without a hood
My family is the best
More than all the rest.

Nathan Tang (10)

This Is Me

This is me.
I am unique and different.
I have a different life and type to others.
I have my own world and life ahead of me.
The other people in this book are different to me.
I like being unique
It means I am different
And have a different and unique view of everything.
This is me.

Safiyyah Abubakar (7)

Who I Am

I am the son of Ketan and Deepti,
I am a boy who strives in anything I do,
I help a person in need
And care for every living being,
I am caring and loving
And sometimes a bit mischievous,
If someone is feeling lonely
My presence cheers them up,
This is how I act and this is me.

Shaylan Patel (11)

Sleeping

When my mum tucks me in,
She makes me feel very thin,
Usually, I'm a sleepyhead,
But sometimes I think
What's under my bed?
I have lots of bad dreams
As you can see,
But sometimes nice ones
With giant ice creams!
It really is no big deal
When I know this is not real.
Right?

Marley Jackson (10)

Me, Me, Me

E very furry tail is my friend.
V ery good at sports.
E very day I wish I had a dog.
L ots and lots of second cousins.
Y es to crisps, yes to music, and yes to cycling.
N o to bananas, no to spiders, and a big no to snakes.

Evelyn Thompson (8)

I-S-S-A

My name is I-S-S-A
And I am four.

I like playing with my friends
Drawing, making, and cooking.

I love to play rugby
And gaming with my brother.

I listen to music
And dance with my sister.

I eat lots of ice cream
And different flavour jelly too.

My name is I-S-S-A
And I am four.

Issa Chowdhury (4)

A Star

You're a star
Star, star
With your light
Shining bright
You flash like a lamp
And fly like a bird
Or when you're looking down
I'm looking up at you
I twinkle just like you
And I look just like you
You really are a star.

Jessica Emberson (7)

Amazon Rainforest Poetry

I can see...
towering trees making shadows on my hand,
monkeys swinging through the trees,
the spotty jaguar hunting its prey,
the green grass growing.

I can hear...
monkeys screaming in trees,
the snakes hissing,
the pandas stomping.

Lucas M (8)

This Is Me

I like to play football every afternoon,
I like eating chocolate cake,
Swimming is also one of my favourite sports,
Playing with my fluffy dog is fun,
I enjoy playing bowling,
Measuring my height is interesting
to see how tall I am,
Going to clubs is very enjoyable.

Aiden Chesler (7)

Autumn

I can see all the orange, yellow, green and brown
leaves falling from the trees
I can hear the birds tweeting in the sky
I can feel the leaves falling from the trees
onto my head
I can taste yummy fruit
I can smell the fireworks banging.

Charlotte Walker (5)

Big Sister, Little Sister

Being the best I can be,
I love my sister, Phoebe.
Guiding her along the way,
Seeing her every day.
Into my room, she comes,
Showing her how to have fun.
Teaching her how to read,
Every time I plant a seed.
Really, it is fun to be
A big sister!

Poppy Cosgrove (7)

This Is Me

I am black,
I am proud,
I am quiet,
Sometimes loud!

I am funny,
I am caring,
I love everyone
I am daring!

This is me,
You are you,
Let's show the world what we can do!

I have finished doing me,
Now it's time...
To get to know you!

Shania Mbaziira (11)

My Life

Life is fun
Life is boring
You can catch me yawning
At 7am in the morning.

I wake up to go to school
But I just want to go in the pool
We do maths
We do science
I just want to read about giants!

Talia Elatta (11)

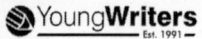

This Is Me

I like dragons but hate dinosaurs
I hate homework but like school
I like fruits but hate vegetables
I hate English but like maths
I like dogs but am terrified of spiders
I hate guitar but like piano
I like walking but hate running.

Minudi Thilakarathna (9)

She's More Than A Girl, She's My Best Friend

- **B** rooke
- **E** njoyable
- **S** tunning
- **T** alented

- **F** riendly
- **R** elatable
- **I** ntelligent
- **E** nchanting
- **N** oisy
- **D** efinitely my best friend.

Ruby Miller-Barratt (11)

Sona

My name is Sona
My favourite colour is red
I like to eat bread
I have a big heart
I help with the shopping cart
I like candy
I am very handy
I am a nice friend
I follow the trend.

Sona Dukkipati (10)

This Is Me

I play football like Harry Kane
I want to play football for England
I am happy like a snowdrop in the winter
I want to be a cool monster truck driver
I like the golden cheese
And red hot pepperoni on my pizza.

Jamie Williams (8)

Cold Days

It is a cold day,
Outside is cold, wet, and grey.
I want a hot cuppa tea,
It's my favourite drink,
So, I won't pour it down the sink!
I want hot noodles,
And maybe some strudels.
It is a cold day.

Maryam Iqbal

This Is Me!

A pinch of friendliness.
A galloon of funny and joyful friends.
A spoonful of enjoyable netball.
A cup of yummy pizza.
A great scoop of yellow, as yellow as the sun.
This is me.

Varenya Sharma (8)

My Hobbies

I am a...
Acro dancer,
Saturday swimmer,
Girl Guider,
Book reader,
Chatty cheerleader,
Animal lover,
Jubilant singer,
Late riser,
Chocolate eater,
Water drinker,
Dog keeper,
Panda adopter.

This is me!

Ilinca Maria Istrati (10)

Guess Who?

A loud talker
A speed walker

A keen rider
A jolly writer

An inquisitive baker
A cake maker

A good singer
A violin stringer

A daydreamer
An ice creamer

A ball kicker
A food picker

This is me!

Aishlinn Garvey (10)

This Is Me

I am as colourful as a rainbow
I am as cute as a kitten
I am as funny as a clown
I am as fast as a cheetah
I am super cool and amazing
I am as tall as the sky.

Aimee Kelly (8)

James

J ames is my name
A lways like to have a cuddle
M y favourite animal is a shark
E very day is very happy
S harky is the best ever toy.

James Mason (7)

I'm Feeling

I'm sad,
I'm happy.
I'm worried,
I'm carefree.
I'm bold,
I'm shy.
I'm hopeful,
I'm unsure.
I'm proud,
I'm meek.
I'm just *me!*

Layla Fitzgerald (8)

This Is Me

This is me
My name is Abby
I am eight years old
I like to be goth
I like to play
I want to dance
I want to run now
This is me
Let me be.

Abby Bassong (8)

Happiness

(A tanka)

Happiness stretches
From people you spend time with
Flowing through bodies
Maybe only for a while
But the memories don't fade.

Jinxuan Chen (11)

Rayne

R unning with my sister
A nd being awesome every day
Y es you know me
N ice and helpful
E very time.

Rayne Lucita (9)

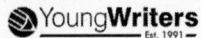

Keishin

There once was a boy called Keishin
Who went to Eastcote Station
He went on a train
To go to White Hart Lane
But ended up at the wrong location!

Keishin Okano (8)

This Is Me!

My heart is as red as a rose
My hair is blonde and brown
I love to play every day
My favourite sport is gymnastics
And this is all about me!

Mia Griffin (9)

I Am Me!

This is me!
I am charismatic
I am confident
I am clever
I am bossy
I am happy
And most importantly I'm me!

Isabelle Seabrook (10)

This Is Me
(A haiku)

Rich, deep, bold brown eyes
Long, silky, straight dark brown hair
Polite and friendly.

David Fleming (11)

A Happy Haiku About Me

I think I am cool
Loving, amazing and kind
That is who I am.

Lola Tash (10)

The Journey Of Love

Tiptoeing through the thick sturdy reeds,
and the silent gasp of willowy trees.
Looping around the whispering lake,
never ever stopping to take a break.
Running through the little town,
and the old camera shop all coloured brown.
Swerving past the lively coffee shop,
and the lights that always told me to stop,
The garden that welcomed all the birds
and the odd little shop
that sold things quite absurd.
Down past the church's vibrant glass pane
and all the way past memory lane.
This beautiful journey symbolises my love,
all for you, caring Mummy dove,
But this specific road trip will never ever end,
for the best time in my eyes,
is the time with you I spend.

Aimee Swart (11)
Alder Hey Children's Hospital, Waterloo

Break The Silence

Walking through the door,
As I stare at the floor,
I hope one day,
The clouds will lift away,

Each morning I wake up,
Trying not to erupt,
The hurt inside,
That dampens my pride,

For five years now,
I have let them allow,
To dim my light,
Stop me shining bright,

Well enough is enough,
It's time to get tough,
The bullies will not win,
I need to fight and sing,

I need to show my true purpose,
To show others they cannot hurt us,
We need to take a knee,
Shout as one. *"This is me!"*

Daisy Adela Anderson (12)
Hassenbrook Academy, Stanford-Le-Hope

YOUNG WRITERS INFORMATION

We hope you have enjoyed reading this book – and that you will continue to in the coming years.

If you're the parent or family member of an enthusiastic poet or story writer, do visit our website www.youngwriters.co.uk/subscribe and sign up to receive news, competitions, writing challenges and tips, activities and much, much more! There's lots to keep budding writers motivated!

If you would like to order further copies of this book, or any of our other titles, then please give us a call or order via your online account.

Young Writers
Remus House
Coltsfoot Drive
Peterborough
PE2 9BF
(01733) 890066
info@youngwriters.co.uk

Join in the conversation!
Tips, news, giveaways and much more!

 YoungWritersUK   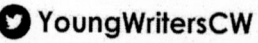 YoungWritersCW    youngwriterscw